Painting the Cat's Vision

by

Alice Elizabeth Rogoff

BLUE LIGHT PRESS ❖ 1ST WORLD PUBLISHING

1ST WORLD
PUBLISHING

SAN FRANCISCO ❖ FAIRFIELD ❖ DELHI

1ST WORLD LIBRARY
PO Box 2211
Fairfield, IA 52556
www.1stworldpublishing.com

BLUE LIGHT PRESS
www.bluelightpress.com
bluelightpress@aol.com

BOOK & COVER ART & DESIGN
Melanie Gendron
melaniegendron999@gmail.com

COVER PHOTO
Alice Elizabeth Rogoff

AUTHOR PHOTO
David H. Williams

FIRST EDITION

Library of Congress Control Number: 2018950997

ISBN 9781421838137

Acknowledgements:

"Immigration" appeared in *Blue Collar Review* Summer 2015, "Green" in the *Weekly Avocet* #146, September 23rd, 2015 and the *Haight Ashbury Literary Journal* Vol. 32 No. 1 2015, "The Village of Mad, Hungary" in *Pacific Media Workers' Newsletter* 2014, Poetrymagazine.com Winter Edition 2013, and *Haight Ashbury Literary Journal* Vol. 29 No. 1 2011, "Burns" in Poetrymagazine.com Anthology, "The Children's Library in *23rd Street Poets* 2009, *Barge Wood* (CC. Marimbo 2012), and Poetrymagazine.com Winter Edition 2013, "Four" in *The Throwback* July 2003, "Out of Milwaukee" in *Poetry at the 33*, 1994 and *Noe Valley Voice* 1989, "Mendocino Night" in *Haight Ashbury Literary Journal* Vol. 33 No. 1 2016, "Lonely" in *Haight Ashbury Literary Journal* Vol. 32 No. 1 2015, "How We Organized" in a broadside funded by the San Francisco Arts Commission 2014,"Strangers" in *Barge Wood* (CC. Marimbo 2012), "My Poems" in *Blue Collar Review* Spring 2017, "The Maple Tree" in *Pudding Magazine* #66 2017, "A Visit to an Old Friend in Minnesota" in *Haight Ashbury Literary Journal* Vol. 34 No. 1 2018, "Disappearing?" in *Caveat Lector* Vol. XXVIII No. 2 Spring 2018, "Visiting Kansas City, Missouri" in *Ambush 6*, 2018.

PAINTING THE CAT'S VISION

TABLE OF CONTENTS

Cuba

A horse gallops
Past the blue
Turquoise water
On a salamander
Shaped island
Into a sunset
That changes
And does not change
Past conversations
From the 1950s,
Mickey Mantle,
Minnie Minoso,
And invasions;
The horse canters around
A horse-drawn carriage
And taxi,
Alongside a glassy hotel.
The horse gallops
With the young,
Trots with
The old,
It wants to dance
New steps or old?
No matter what,
The music
Keeps playing.

A horse gallops
Around a salamander
Shaped island,
On city streets
Along a turquoise

Shore,
Carrying both the
Past and
The future;
The hooves
Click out the
Music of clave;
The year could be
1880, 1959, 2017,
A small band
Is everywhere,
A young woman
Is singing
In the heat.

Eire North

It was very peaceful
in Derry
that day
we toured the walled city of Derry.
We wanted to go to Northern Ireland.
We went hiking at the Giants' Causeway.
I joked that was the most dangerous part of our trip.
Maybe it was too quiet in Derry
by the memorials in Gaelic for those killed by the British
and You are Entering Free Derry sign.
There were no passers-by.
Our tour
which included Muslims and Jews
and Protestants,
climbed up the walls —
noticing on Derry's Protestant side,
"We will never surrender."
I wore blue.
Back in Dublin, I'd wear
green again.
I left my orange shoes
home.
Perhaps, the truce was
working.
The next day, the British
apologized for Bloody Sunday.
Reconciliation is not an easy word
to understand.
From the cliffs at
The Giants' Causeway were
one hundred and sixty-four steps.
I thought that was the

most dangerous path in our journey.
It's harder to walk up than
down, our guide said.
But walking up or down is
hard when one is afraid of
heights.
When we got to the famous rocks
we realized we could have
taken a bus or a short walk
to reach them.
But then we would not have
gotten the view.
The beautiful green cliffs,
the brown earth,
the turquoise sea.
July Twelfth —
The "Orange" Protestants parade in a
Catholic section of Belfast.
The people for a united Ireland protest.
There are flames across
our morning newspaper.
That view from the walls.
It seemed too quiet.

Visiting Kansas City, Missouri

The little red diner,
Barbecue and
Benches, noon sun
People come up and talk,
Running backwards
Gazing over a bridge
To find a river,
Sunken steamboat,
An ambiguous slave or free state,
Union or Confederacy.
Nearby Ferguson, Black Lives Matter.
Saturday night,
In front of the Blue Room Jazz Club,
Couples of all kinds stroll on the sidewalk,
Chatting with strangers.
Mansions near the
Asian Art Museum.
Taxi drivers who
Ask for directions,
By a hotel, mattresses carried away
On the top of taxies
By taxi drivers.
A stocky white eleven year old boy
Happily jogs around the bases
Of the Negro Leagues Baseball Museum's diamond
By statues of Josh Gibson and Satchel Paige.
We all seem to get along
But people keep asking why we are here.

Burns

Burns
On her face
Even though she survived.
Her burns still mark her body.
The demonstrators are walking
Down Market Street,
Going to the GAP store,
The Walmart R Us workers
Join in the march
Starting from Local 2 Hotel and Restaurant Employees Union.
The cable car tourist crowds
Are in front of us,
The sign on the GAP window,
Life is Shorts
On a hot day
In San Francisco.
Two women lie down
As the dead.
Women shoppers ask me questions.
Women from Bangladesh speak,
Say the names of those
Who died
In the garment factory fire
In Bangladesh.
Friends lost.
Burns
Under the skin
That do not disappear.

How We Organized — 1930s

Jennie said,
We met
At our homes
Away from the job
So did we said Marion Brown Sills,
  Marion Brown Sills called us,
     Jennie Matyas came to our apartments
In Chinatown
During the Depression
The workers
In garment factories
Would meet clandestinely
     Department store workers were like that too,
Said Marion,
Mostly women,
Yes.
Jennie was Hungarian,
Once a garment worker in New York,
In San Francisco,
She got home after midnight to help organize.
So Ko Lee
Sewed buttonholes during the day,
Then went to the San Francisco Labor Council
For the Chinese Ladies' Garment Workers' Union.
Marion said the garment workers can use my office,
Me too, said Carmen Lucia from the Hatmakers Union.
It was how we organized.
There were three, then there were three-thousand.

My Poems

My poems,
Like Grandma Ida's
Handicrafts,
Trimmings,
They were called
To accessorize
A blouse or a dress.
In her nineties,
She made doilies
At production level,
Like in her first years
As a widow
Making do
In the early years
Of Social Security
Accumulating
A little bit
That she would later receive.
Each poem
Like a crocheted
Embroidered, knitted
Small tchotchke.
The pen in the hand
On paper
Like a needle
On cloth.

Immigration

Some people disappear
At night,
Some during the day,
Even in the union,
ICE asking for papers.
Going back to Mexico.
Deportees.
I saw whole families and
Half families
Go,
Mothers without
Their children,
Children without
A mother,
Four years of
Scrubbing a floor,
Or making beds,
Then, they were
Gone,
Back to over the
Border,
The wind blows
Between lines on
A map.

How Could They Kill Lorca?

How can one kill a poet?
Their words like blood
Spilling on the ground?
Their songs
Filling the air up to the clouds.
How can one point a bullet
At one who speaks of love?
How can one trample
On beauty and music —
Las palabras and flamenco,
Green and wild horses,
Mountain flowers
Blooming on icy mountains
Falling into a crevasse
The fascists on a firing squad
How can one —

Louise, Tillie, Kazmi, Alice, and Jan

Jan Cook guides Louise Gilbert
to the City College art show,
takes Louise from the On Lok senior residence
in North Beach.
Louise was Refregier's assistant
on his WPA murals.
Louise sits and gazes
at seventy years of her own work.

Tillie Olsen reads poems
behind a podium at the Women's Building.
Ninety years old,
dressed in a black skirt and blue shawl,
she stands
for her entire reading.
Murals of women hug the building.

Jan Cook stands on a ladder
to paint the mural on
Thurgood Marshall High School,
A montage of the Bayview district.
Six feet tall and
short cropped blonde hair.

Jan sorts Louise Gilbert's art
and hangs the show,
and takes Louise home
when all the students and guests have left
after four hours.

I introduce Tillie Olsen
at City Lights Bookstore,
the poems on garment workers,
the 1934 General Strike,
being a mother.
The audience is all the way down
the second story staircase.

Kazmi Torii creates
the LaborFest brochure.
She works in her home office,
stacked with videos and books, and folders.
She learned layout
in a City College class.
Kazmi slides pictures and words
on her computer screen
and types in
"Louise, Tillie, Alice, and Jan."

Working in San Francisco

Streets intersecting,
Looping around hills,
Containing life
From nine to five,
Or two in the morning,
Or twenty-four hours.
On library shelves,
Books do not usually hide from a page;
In hospital corridors,
Blood runs into a vial,
Wheels rotate
One in the morning,
In the rain,
Sun on the bus windows.
Music stands
Lit behind
Reams of notes,
Under symphony chandeliers.
Tired on a bus,
Mattie, twenty-one,
Her hair dyed purple,
On a phone —
Not a dream boss,
Talk to a shop steward.
Home with dishes
And a cat to feed.
Lucky not to be sick,
Or Ellis Act evicted.
Can pay a bill tomorrow
Or the rent next week.
Spend an hour on a union picket line,
Go to a union meeting.
Last week's depression going away.
Have dinner with friends in a café.

Negative Tide

August summer,
a day
of a negative tide,
pulled by the moon and the sun,
to be especially low,
the sea pinned back,
exposing the undersea rock.
I creep onto the seaweed,
tenuously walk from
tide pool to tide pool,
on Hiroshima Day.
Along slippery green
sheaves of green,
starfish, their thick arms
clinging to the rocks,
the kaleidoscope worlds of
sea urchins and fish in each round pond,
an uncovering of the unseen
animals and plants of the sea.
The waves come flowing in fast
rushing over the beautiful newfound world
gone in a moment.

Reconstruction

Round houses
Disappear
Into the earth,
Creating their own images,
And shadows
Under that spot;
The steady roots of these buildings
Could have stayed and stayed
But condominiums ignored them
Replacing round houses
On shifting deserts
In Southern California.
Now, only memories
Of a native
Standing alone
On the new road,
Seeing circles
That housed her spirit.

The Train Across Canada

The train
Veering and winding
Through the mountain paths
The train drops down steep inclines

The tamaracks
Pines that change from green to gold
Shivers of needles
Translating

The frost
Settling

Through the window
The moon
Like a white dog
Howls melodiously
We sing softly to ourselves

Beyond the mountain paths
A native village
Beyond my sight.

Do Dolphins Wish?

Do dolphins know
Us (humans) laughing
Women, men, sliding
On skateboards
Singers in the park,
Cayman Islands
Investors, Sunset
Scavengers truck
Drivers, Marta
Doing her nails,
Lisa pregnant, wheeling
Twins;
Do dolphins think
About us,
(Humans, Homo
Sapiens) Did they
Notice when monkeys
Became human?
Do they wonder at
Boats that invaded
Their seas?
Do dolphins hate us
As they leap to
Socialize,
We killing
Them,
Trapping
Them,
Eating
Their flesh,

Devouring
The
Smiling
Mammals?
Do dolphins
Sing when
We (the
Humans) are
Asleep
Hear cats,
Dogs, parakeets,
Golden fish?
Do dolphins
Wish?

Stations

If we could take trains
Backwards to where we
Were born,
To where we came from,
Pulling into a welcoming
Depot;
Find the right station
For the day or night.
Maybe, the ornate gilded one.
The only palace we can all partake of,
Or the tiny way station
With friendly people
For a train
Going up into the mountains,
Or the suburban one,
Jamaicans and Irish-Americans
Standing in line at the little ticket booth
Figuring the schedules,
Commuters looking to go to larger cities.
That slice of terminal,
Embryonic,
Returns you to a bubble
Back in time,
For anyone who has left
Their station,
For stations
That are still left.

The Village of Mad, Hungary

Mad,
My grandmother's birthplace.
There are wells and wine cellars.
The wells are covered.
There is running water
in the houses now.
No falling deep into
a tunnel
like Alice in Wonderland
discovering.
We walked
in the heat
through the village
with grapes on the hillsides.
The triangular huts
are wine cellars,
one to a home.
Tokaji Classico.
Hand pumped fountains.
Drink me.
News of the village
each morning on a loudspeaker.
The guide to the old synagogue
only speaks Hungarian,
points to a wall of names,
says one word —
Auschwitz.
Colors swirl in stars
on the ceiling above our heads.
The synagogue sits on a hill
viewing the town,

being viewed
like a prima donna.
A key from an unseen man
lets us in the gate
of the 18th century cemetery.
Grandma visited an aunt aged one hundred and three
in nineteen-twenty.
Names in Hebrew.
A quiet piece of paper
on a squeaky gate
has a Brooklyn phone number to call.
The lady from restoring cemeteries
in Brooklyn,
says only first names used.
What was her name?
A cat in the road.
Who are you?
Alice.

Four

Four grandparents
From different countries
At least to begin with
The part of Russia my
Grandfather was from
With a change of borders,
Is now Belarus,
My grandmother's family,
I thought was from
Poland, but now I'm
Told it's Lithuania,
Grandpa Morris was
From the Austro-Hungarian
Empire, so he was Hungarian,
But now, the city is in Czechoslovakia,
Now, in Slovakia:
Grandma Ida only
Suffers from confusion,
Being further east
Than I believed
Shifting
Imagination and
Perceptions of who
One is or was,
At any specific time in
History, speaking
The language that
Was correct, and
Being Hungarian
But with a Germanic
Name — somehow
How did that occur?

Historical crosscurrents
Rise and ebb,
I don't understand
Ethnic cleansing
Would never separate
My parts —
I would have to be
Quartered,
Boiled, puréed,
And when would the
Map of myself dry out?

Floating

Those were the days,
Taking youthful
Steps in the Catskills,
In summer camps.
Where one could
Woo easily,
Drifting softly
In a row-
Boat, on
A calm lake,
Simple pleasures
Like sour cream and beets,
During a Depression,
When one's
Future was
Around the
Bend in
The lake, in
The faraway
Purple of
The sunset.

The Maple Tree

The maple's sap was always sticky,
oozing out of a soft spot on the tree bark.
I was always caught on it,
like in a web,
pulled to that wrong spot,
fingers, hair, wool winter sweater.
Maples further north had syrup.
We had a spot to avoid.
The skirt of fall amber leaves
beneath the trunk
flared like a round fifties skirt
that one could spin around in
like a Sufi, or sit on
like a magic carpet.
Being a child in the nineteen-fifties,
a little sap, bucolic.
Particles tiny sticky
stuck.
Stevenson with a hole in his shoe,
and McCarthy trials on TV
at four in the afternoon.

Home and Garden

Home,
more than a sleeping bag
tucked under a doorway.
Less
less than a mansion
or a castle in Spain.
Going home,
more than a hot air vent,
Less than
a condo in the sky.
A garden of Christmas trees
to wander through,
needles falling through
one's fingers,
the smell of pine
clinging to old clothes.
Garden for those in backpacks
on the Civic Center lawn.
Golden Gate Park and a shopping cart.
Glossy pages of *Home and Garden* magazine
covering a head
in the rain.
Homer looking
for a ship
lost in a storm
on highway islands.
Home and garden.
Mas y menos,
More and less.

Disappearing?

One can slip in between the cracks. One can fly away like fuzz on a dandelion or become wild like a poppy. One can blend with the drops of dew. If one is alone on a bus that drives through the night passing signs that one cannot always see, only a few lights completely visible, one can disappear from one's friends who stop looking, without a lantern, or a few railings to hold onto, above a canyon, above a canyon without a railing to hold onto.

The Ermine Girl

Face ermine white
so pale to blend
into her winter.
She took the name Snow
because she needed
something pretty
and a name was free.
Runaway street girl,
curled in a doorway,
once her name was Sarah.
Her white mask
could be a death mask
or could be the soft
white mammal running
unseen through
ice fields and tundra, through
life's most northern reaches.
Her pale face like milk,
a balloon on the corner
blown above birches, and light poles,
sometimes sweet like sugar.

Earthquakes

At the foster group home,
in the Ingleside
on the night of the earthquake,
six teenagers were
under the back porch
as the porch
rocked and the
lights went out
hill after hill.
Then for several hours
the counselor Dan
drove them in
virtual darkness,
crisscrossing the
Bayview and Hunters Point,
ferrying them to Double Rock
and to the Sunnydale Projects
because all the teenagers
wanted to find family.
Once he even drove down
my street
as I sat with
a candle.
Then, all the teenagers went back
to the temporary home,
to the aftershocks
that would linger
for months.

Beverly (Anne)

Beverly (stage name Anne) lived in the Granada Resident Hotel
On the edge of the Tenderloin.
She came to my Senior drama group,
But she was more than amateur,
She still had her Screen Actors Guild membership.
She had played Blanche when young.
We talked about Birdie in *The Little Foxes*.
She registered for a talent agency
And I saw her on television shows.
Playing a dingy cantankerous old woman,
A speaking part, more pay than a walk-on.
Her beauty hardly recognizable.
She collected residuals when the reruns ran.
Living in her one room hotel room
She rehearsed her comedy routines
Sitting on her one chair,
Facing the three cranberry glass wine glasses
That she'd kept from a former home,
And photos of her three sons when young.
She'd acted with the Pasadena Playhouse.
Her *Rebecca*'s housekeeper monologue
Could frighten an audience.
Somehow, she'd ended up in San Francisco.
Her Screen Actors Guild card still up to date.

The Old Country

Before she died in America,
She went mad,
Perhaps all history hides
In our minds,
And in the saddest moments,
The psyches open:
She was running
In the streets again,
In Yugoslavia
During the War,
Running out the door there
And the door here,
Gone mad
With that madness,
Fifty years in America,
But her death
Brought her back
To the Old Country.

Cans

She comes on recycling day.
Usually.
At night,
I think she thinks I cannot see her.
She's not invisible.
Her pole balances on her shoulders.
Two bags tied to each end of the pole.
She scavenges quickly.
If I speak to her
she will say she doesn't speak English.
Today is not a recycling day.
There are no cans today.
Has she wandered
onto the wrong road?
When I see her,
she begins to sing
in a low tone.
It sounds like wooo-wooo—
in a language
I do not understand.
She backs off slowly.
For five cents a can,
does it help her family?
Is she destitute?
Her hair is black without gray,
but her age is indecipherable.
I have seen her for years,
disappearing I do not know where.
On the regular recycling days,
she does not sing.

Why My Neighbors Fix Cars

This week,
It's another one,
Lifted off its wheels,
The hood open,
A long and short body underneath,
Smells emanating
Into my doorway,
Motor oil and brake fluid,
Garage door raised,
Engine running,
Pre-2000s,
Only manual
Maybe a business,
Or a favor for a friend,
Or a trade for
Another favor,
Father and son,
During the summer months,
Another car,
A red truck,
Wires yellow and blue sticking out,
The same car
Returning for the
Third time,
I don't think they
Ever get fixed,
Because my
Neighbors fix cars.

Dreaming

Behind a window
Are the faces of three women
Like they are behind a thick red curtain,
Or an orange pot from Central America.
Like they have wound themselves in wool.
Statues on a frieze
On a gritty Chicago Near North storefront window.

Is that window what I will walk through
To come into their world?
High cheekbones
Mesmerized by sad guitars,
Grainy fingers to search a palm.
One of the women has fallen asleep.
The other women's shoulders support her.

Lost in my dreams
I pass by the three Gypsy women,
Dreaming
Behind the storefront glass.

Searching for Dolphins

I'm looking for more than dolphins,
maybe a new hat
or a prize in a poetry contest,
a day without bills,
a city supervisor I like
who votes
to keep Seniors in their homes.
Those waves could be dolphins,
their noses above water
giving glimpses
of life on the coast,
still swimming by
I think, or hope.
Those dark moons
could be dolphins.

Maine Song: Living in the Maine YWCA

Jill always working
As a waitress
In the supermarket
I miss Jill
And Teddy
Driving around on
Cold nights
Around a cold
Island
Waiting for the car
To freeze or a
Snow to fall
Making payments
On the car
Or getting a new job
The slow Maine
Summer then
Going by Going by
For us all us all
In winter,
Driving around on
Dark cold roads
Never knowing when
The snow
Would stop us, or the law,
The law,
On such a little island,
One runs out of space,
One has only so many
Places to go, to go
On those cold snowy
Nights and hot summers,

I think of Teddy
And Jill, of Teddy and
Jill,

I miss Jill and her strange
Sunny smile, so broad
Going out with the
Man from California
Was it real? Was it
Real?
He knew everything
That one could know,
One could know.

And of all those songs I
Sung
Of all those songs

You could hear them all
Way down the hall,
Jill said, all the way
Down the hall.

Out of Milwaukee

It looks like
Milwaukee
I remember
Her saying.
The upper Noe Valley.
The kids at St. Paul's.
German bakeries.
Well, it's a feeling
Of being back
Home —
Her face
As though framed in
The lace from an antique shop.
She didn't really
Know there was a
Section of town like
That in San Francisco. She
Bought a book
Of poems from a
Used bookstore
Went through the
National Geographics for
A half hour.
I've got her
Picture now I
Thought, sketching
It in my mind
But it bled, like
Watercolor
Why was she so
Fragile

Milwaukee, I
Thought was beer
And Oktoberfest
Looking back,
All those church steeples,
In every neighborhood
High above the
Houses,
As my car mirrored
The town behind me
Along the highway,
Down to Chicago,
Back to San Francisco.

Hannah

She is living in a house
Too small for her;
Tall, angular
She breaks the walls
With her elbows
The walls are what irritate her.
She is a dancer
Who breathes softly
She is molasses, pine sap
She is never at rest,
Always moving;
She is a healer
Her hands are swans,
She sews herself into a bundle
To swing over her shoulder;
She is a dance
That moves with her
Back to the room.
The room is too small for her,
She dances with her eyes.

Mendocino

Four women lived in the house
By the sea gate
Danielle was pregnant
And was crying each night
For a child she didn't
Want to have.
Janie, the weaver, took in the wild sea cats
Who lived off of the sea salt air
And fights at night.
Holly was a waitress,
And in-between tables
She tumbled in bedclothes
Of lace.
May was a sailor who
Fell in love with a young man
Who read Irish folk tales
Each night.
The house, full of old stuff,
Leaked and was
Warm only on sunny days.
It was turning on its own
Feet,
And overrun with cats
And Danielle's
Abortion.

Mendocino Night

As night lay over the Pacific, a light was left burning, Elizabeth's porch light, shedding a yellow glow over a very small space, the whole town enfolding itself like a California poppy, drawing in, protected, the horse that was to be found in the morning fallen through a footbridge, its legs dangling two feet above a stream, (it stumbling in the darkness, the bridge splitting beneath its weight, the splinters shattering into the arms of someone else's nightmare) the cats screeching to each other in the early morning hours of the horse's solitude, the sunrise slowly diminishing all other lights except a forest fire burning seven miles away, "contained," the radio said, "contained," by a circle of two hundred men, one hundred and fifty acres of timber burned, the calls of roosters rising into a chorus, the people coming into town and parked outside the market waiting for it to open at nine, vans and mud-splattered pick ups full of shovels, carpenters' tools, inevitably a dog, at least one window or door handle in each pick up broken and never repaired, one other car found left by the side of the road, and starting to be stripped like piranha strip a cow, only not as lightning fast, with a slowness born of time going on; and the men coming to get the horse exactly as Mrs. Gibney is telling of it to Anita in the market; and as the shops of town open for another day of business, (the rope around the horse's neck a lesser trap than the bridge) the horse is gradually led home, the fire put out, *"contained,"* the radio said, *"contained,"* the day spreading its wings like an effortless hawk, a light waiting another day for night to return, waiting for the sun to drop into the ocean like a petal.

The Great Highway

At sunset, I arrange my life
At the Great Highway,
Kicking my shoes off,
Letting them sink into the
Sand.
Facing off the wind,
Giving up,
And becoming one with it,
Trying to light a match
Without the flame
Blown out,
Rearranging the debris of bonfires,
Graffiti and lumber
Into a collage,
The sun is like music,
Glowing and glowing,
The old piers
Disintegrating,
Inviting one to climb
On them.
Knowing if you did, you
Might fall through, or
Not.

Strangers

I keep taking the train at night,
the underground one,
with my fellow denizens,
the signs flashing minutes
and where we are destined to go.
Teens lean against walls.
A rat scurries down the tracks.
The lady-next-to-me's good eyes
catch its gray body that
matches the metal.
We talk about rats
we have seen before,
and cats, and our lives
while waiting for the train at night,
hundreds of feet below ground,
two people who will
never see each other again.

Fillmore Street

Meanderings into the light of jazz nights,
Fillmore street alleys,
Jam for a few hours,
With a jazz great from the street,
Or a drummer that never made it home,
Or a jazz ghost that sits in to play.

.

The Moonlight Woman

The woman with the high
Cheekbones,
High heels,
Leather coat,
Wafting down the
Lanes of San Francisco,
Into an alley,
Fashioning her hair
Above the bones,
Bones of a tribeswoman,
Like the curve of the moon,
And her hand,
She disappears down
The urban mountain
Road,
Into a tiny store
With roots and herbs,
Aromas are gathered
Into bags and taken
Away with her,
Drunk in teas,
Under a skylight
By moonlight.

Diane Di Prima's Class

She is swaying, swaying,
    She is tilting, swaying
(the clock stored in the basement
    ringing at intervals)
She is half-woman and half seal.

She is the mirror room in the fun house.

(lost on slanted floors, the
peal of a boat passing through
brain cells)

She is swaying, swaying,
 The bell rings out

The Javanese cats lick their fur.

Down the slide into the glass

pool at the bottom.

The Jazz Woman

The jazz woman
Dances on the piano keys
Her fingers clothed
In silk scarves
Glides on the music
I keep losing her
In deceptive cadences,
Her notes cartwheel,
Somersault through
The music tone
Poems —
She is me
On deep blue
Mornings,
B flats and
Blues notes that
No one can find,
She's got glitter
And lace
And a black dress
With sleeves that
Serrate sound.
She's all alone with
Her music, her
Sheets of paper,
Her ink, her strings,
Chasing notes
That are only hers.

Micheline Alley —on the theme of "The American Dream."

In San Francisco,
there are streets
named for artists,
dancers and poets,
Isadora Duncan
and Ferlinghetti.
Jack Micheline,
poet of the streets,
has a stairway,
not very noticeable.
Wandering the streets,
I find the lovely stairway
tucked back in North Beach
for Jack who died on a train.
Micheline Alley though small and hidden
commemorates better
than the streets for Presidents
Polk and Taylor
who claimed Mexican and Native land,
or Justin Herman Plaza
for the leader of urban renewal
destroying a black neighborhood.
Perhaps Jack could have gotten a stairway
when he was alive
and could have sat there
and written his long rambling poems.
Micheline Alley,
a good place to dream,
named for a poet who lived in alleys
and died on a train.

The Children's Library

The library
Had been an icehouse,
Ice carried from nearby ponds,
Smooth cold blocks
Instead of books,
In a dollhouse-like cottage
In the park,
A remnant
Where my child
Lingered to
Melt,
To become transformed
Carried on the stream
Or over the bridge.
Then, it was changed again.
The books were carted away like ice blocks.
The library became a deserted little house
Freezing in winter without books.
I ran from water rats
In the streams,
Until the cracked shades were lifted,
As the library was brought back,
And the children moved in once more
With unicorns,
And dragons,
And the nice ghosts
Of my childhood
Along a new flowing stream.

Lonely?

Is she lonely?
She who sits alone at the counter
Sipping tea
Reading her book,
One hour disappearing
Like into a train tunnel,
Time and time again,
She returns
To the stool in the corner,
She might smile
Or have a face almost tearful,
If she were a cat, she
Would be a lost kitten
Found on a street
Under a car
On a rainy night,
One little mew
Saying I am here.
One day, she's gone
Then here again,
Then finally gone
Moved away to another city,
Another state,
Or unexpected sickness,
Empty spaces
At the counter,
Then, was she ever there?
How does loneliness linger
When the lonely are
    Gone?

Me

There's the girl
Who can't do math,
Who daydreams in algebra,
Drawing little pictures,
Doodles,
Wishes she'd brought
Colored pencils,
And pays no attention,
And there's the girl
Who one day
Realizes that
Calculus will tell her
Where the stars go,
How a building will not lean,
So she could make
A beautiful building,
Be like Maya Lin
And understand
How to design
A memorial for
The war that
Drowned out
Her teenage and
Young adult years.
How one day
There's the girl
Who understands
What she didn't
Ever understand.
A teacher said
She was "hopeless,"

While another
Said she was talented.
All in the same girl,
Me. Drifting
Maybe drifted.
Then not.
Like that lonely cloud
Moved to a dock,
Sometimes, we
Don't understand,
Sometimes,
Understanding
Comes.

My Turtle

My turtle
helps me to see,
a small magnifying glass,
with the shell around the glass
and legs

People are fond
of the turtle
I suppose
like people pet
a companion dog,

Though they are not supposed to.
Its head does not hide in its shell.
Two of its legs are broken off,
making it look like it is swimming,
more companion than plain glass,
Native Americans say the earth was
created on a turtle's back,

In Golden Gate Park,
the turtles sleepily nod
as one rows past.

Opposite Ends of the Spectrum

Is it a matter of going
Lighter or darker,
Youth and age,
Immortality or finality,
What my eggs are doing,
Darkly mysterious to me;
Like the center of a volcano,
The womb,
Grandmother was old when
She had my mother,
A cousin, an only child,
Was born when her mother
Was in her forties,
By forty-five,
Life is starting to end
Or could still be beginning,
I count my days
Like with an abacus,
Watch the moon and sun exchange places,
See the entire
Spectrum rise like a
Rainbow over my head.

Geometry Problem

White wolves
Howl on blank pages
On Montana mornings
And California switchbacks.
Coyotes roam
Urban hills,
Lovers roll in the snow
Creating angels.
Angels fly in the treetops,
And sometimes I'm happy
As the night wraps
Its arms around stars and me.

Protecting the Center

To prevent being struck
by lightning
you need to stand with
your legs together;
with your legs
apart, you will
be like a conductor
channeling strokes into
your center;
displacing the
flashover effect
will keep away strikes —
only grazing exterior outer parts,
non vital organs;
and in cold,
when you start to freeze,
nature protects
the center,
taking the
extremities,
the feet, or
hands first.

I stand with the feet
apart;
the lightning
penetrates
the center,
the heart,
and lungs,

like I am a tuning fork
reverberating
in the vital
places;
a fatal problem:
standing open
on an open
plain.

Spinning

Little girl
Going to be a woman
Dancing and spinning
In the space that is
Still yours.

Rebecca

One day, we wondered
why Rebecca
came to school
sad, one day,
not sad the
day
before,
and one day,
she stayed
sad
for ten years,
one day
for ten
years,
Rebecca
sat in
the corner,
her hems
down
around
her heels,
one day,
Rebecca
looked out
the windows
that opened
with poles
like javelin
lances,
one day
Rebecca dropped
a Hebrew

book on
the floor
and kissed
it when
she picked
it up,
one day
children started
 laughing at her
sadness
and her religion,
one day that
lasted ten
years; in
high school
Rebecca began
to smile,
the sorrow
seeking some
other child's
soul,
one day
I asked the teacher,
"What's the
matter with
Rebecca?" and the
teacher answered,
one day
for years,
"Rebecca's mother
died yesterday,"
and Rebecca
always looked
tilted in
those class

pictures, ten
years of
class pictures,
five by eight
in glossy unfoldable
color, ten
years of class
pictures,
One day.

A Visit to an Old Friend in Minnesota

It has been ten years
Since each person on the
Street was coming
For you.
My friend Moira and I walk casually,
In the countryside,
The field beneath our feet,
Frozen swampy footsteps,
And Moira tells me about
Streets with overhangs
To keep out the cold,
And how the wind makes it colder;
I have a scarf winding
Around my neck
To fire away the chill.
Moira goes to the hospital for her pills,
Tablets of thorazine.
We remember we had been to dances together,
And, on vacation, had climbed fire towers.
We pass a forest of pines,
Can breathe their scent,
Try to forget about fires burning faraway.

The Nervous Breakdown

1.   The Nervous Breakdown

All the words
You never bled
Coring and pulling
The lips apart,
Welling like oil
Over birds and fish
And thornless flowers,
I held
Your shoulders
And felt
The frail blades
Break —
Two puzzles
Like chandeliers
In labor.
When you left,
A knotted candle
Took your place.

2.   **The Hospital**

Nurses,
Constant
With charts,
Forms to fill out,
Beds
To fill in.
People
Root
Like turnips
Yellow as ice.
Each hallway
Speaks hungry,
Wishful.
The walls
Are white;
Your words
Are enamel.

Mary

Mary sat as though
A Child's Garden of Verses
were within her,
and a sad guitar
under a purple hat,
a wake in a Joyce novel,
a winding street through Jerusalem,
clad in black,
with her cane,
and shawl,
light blue eyes faded,
toothless, and long white hair,
Mary comes to our rehearsals,
and sits in a corner,
and speaks to herself. Her
iridescence shines like a light on a hillside
early in the morning.

An Engineer

My father was
good at
untangling knots
in chains
that dangled
around necks,
or hoses that
crisscrossed
lawns.
He tried to keep
parts straight
on windblown
hairdos,
keep patterns
that went awry
straight, keeping children's
emotions
and his
in neat bureaus,
in desk drawers
under control,
but as he grew
old,
people told him their problems
and went to him for advice,
because he
was the only
one who
knew how
to untie
the knots.

Douglas

I met him on a bus ride
I was shy
And wore yellow
Leanings,
He was troubled
About something
And he was funny,
He was there
By accident
Perhaps the
Best way
To meet
Your friends
And as the Massachu-
Setts border
Ran beneath
Our feet,

I was no good at
Explaining
That he couldn't
Come over
Not because he was black
And I was white,
But because
I was ashamed
Of my own family,
All the crazy
Screamings,
And no place
Ever to go,
Even a bus ride —
A sanctuary.

And never knowing
What it is to be liked
Didn't know
What to do
About it.
In the seat that I usually
Reserved for
Paper bags.

The Crab Apple Tree

I liked to climb up
the backyard crab apple tree
with the fruit too
small and bitter to eat,
nestle in-between the two arms.
It was a little climb,
not as high as a very athletic
child could go,
the trunk's skin beginning to crackle,
a cranky tree
like a perpetually annoyed relative
who was kind secretly.
After all the other trees were cut down,
the crab apple was still there,
probably forgotten,
not as troublesome or as beautiful,
letting one dream a little
but not wildly,
never high
enough to
crash.

Green

The limbs in the plum tree
Are lower.
I'd forgotten to check for plums,
Now, by the lack of red globes
I know the plums are
Not ripe yet.
The small round green fruit
Dots the branches,
Low enough to reach by hand
They look like green apples.
I like this intermediate time
Of greenness
When all I can do is wait;
When the hue is incongruous to its
Red, it stays
Untouched, as
Saying, not yet,
Let me tease you,
For more days
(than you know)
I'm green,
Just wait.

Between Being a Lover and a Friend

Th
e space between
being a friend
and being a lover —
it's the air
between branches
of a tree.
I rode on the
sea with you,
but she explored caverns,
She saw blue,
I saw red,
You were my past,
she was the future.
I knew a clown,
but he saw tears,
like kaleidoscopically
splintering
into many selves,
things one of you
will never know.

Mock Turtle

It was the mock turtle
Sitting in a pool
Of his own tears
Like the ocean.
If we separate,
The turtle comes out again
That hard shell,
Like a room
With a closed door —
Oh mock turtle,
I wish I could
Make you smile.

Love

Love is a spiral
Winds around
Comes back to
Tap from behind,
Curls cozily,
Tightens and squeezes,
And retreats
Letting you breathe,
Love is like a wand,
Touches you gently and
Lets you see showers of
Meteors at midnight,
Puts you on a plane
And wakes you in
Istanbul,
And love is like an old
Coat on a homeless
Person, lying in a doorway,
In foggy drizzle,
It is old and heavy
And warm when
All else is cold.

Love Like Fire

(to be read in two parts)

My lover, like

Blown fire

                              in the center of my
                                  chest

twisted rainbows

                              is a lake

  orange nights
orange time

                              on fire

wet fire

                              the moon
                              a white bird

Fire suspended

                              with wings

  off
the earth

                              on fire

The Rain after Eight Years of Drought

Turning back
into being
that Northwest
where you go
only if you
can cling
to the skin
of a wet tree,
live inside a hole
in the bark,
or navigate
in the fog
on a little boat
in the mist.
The Northwest is
rain rain
for months upon months,
making us
climb inside
tree trunks
and shake
the wet off
like
feathers
and skin slippery
like apple peels.

I don't think
the Northwest
is the sun
drying everything
to a powder.

It is
that renewal
each year
drenching
your fingertips,
making an ordinary street
into a slice of a mountaintop.
It changes how you love.
You love like wishing
for all things warm
and you live on the
edge of a threat,
the danger of being
swept away
by a flood.
And inside, love
eating away to
the core,
the hidden spot
inside you,
while the totem masks
on the outside
fly above the trees
and sing like
eagles and
gray mourning
doves.

In the Canyons

I love back canyons
The desert crevices
The holy places,
Like arriving at an
Altar.
The high walls
Rising above,
But I fear the
Sudden violence
Of the flash flood
After the dry sunlight.

There is the tenseness
Of outwitting
A storm,
Of escaping
The flow of
Waters,
How I could be
Climbing above
An instant flood of
Memories, and
Unprovoked
Anger, a rush
Of cool
In the heat of the
Desert,
Potential death,
Potential life-giving
As new flowers rise.

Canvas

Painters know that the sky
Is a great canvas,
They find light
In their brushes,
Find the sunsets
In their fingers,
The sun rises
With their strokes,
But the sky itself
Will never stay framed.
It falls over the corners
Of square worlds
Changing constantly
At the edges,
Which are not edges
But centers to
Another community
Over the next horizon,
But the painter
Picks up a canvas
And carries it home,
Feeling the sky
Has sung a song
For her to keep.

Point Lobos — Wildlife Sanctuary

               i stand
on the coast of California
this nesting place
     wild birds surround me
and Bellowing
     the sea is rusty apple-green
and churning by the rocks,
     the wind lifts me out over this
               spit of land
     forever
       say the birds coming
          together,
this bright sanctuary,
     forever   say the trails
leading back into the forest,
     and beyond,
       traceable footsteps
               screech
                  the
          sky.

River Islands

1.

    River islands
    Remember
    Rare things
    Moving things
    The silence
    And the sway.

2.

    They crouch
    Current-bound,
    Patient collectors
    On an
    Incandescent
    Shore.

3.

    They weave dreams
    Like driftwood,
    Like stars
    Falling
    In an
    Unanswered
    Question.

4.

    One bird,
    A river-bird,
    One tree,
    An island-tree;
    Each curved
    In shady chapel,
    Their liquid angle
    The night's
    Last look.

Sesshu

Sesshu's
black lines,
inking leaves,
limbs of trees
white spaces,
painting in a circle
snow on paper,
snowfall on paper,
feeling of harmony
in the winter sky.

Sesshu: Fifteenth Century Japanese Zen monk and artist.

Painting the Cat's Vision

Balancing on heights

Inaccessible to me,

Views of my own life and yard

That I do not see —

If I paint from

The cat's perspective,

I try for the spirals of the

Eye, the teetering, the

Search for balance.

About the Author

Alice Elizabeth Rogoff's poetry book *Mural* won a Blue Light Book Award in 2004. Another poetry book, *Barge Wood*, was published by CC.Marimbo in 2012. She has been published in the anthologies *River of Earth and Sky* (Blue Light Press), *It's All Good* and *Your Golden Sun Still Shines* (Manic D Press), *Walking Through a River of Fire: One Hundred Years of Triangle Fire Factory Poems*, and *Poets 11*. Her poetry has been published in many literary magazines including *Borderlands* and *Gyst*. She received a Cultural Equity grant from the San Francisco Arts Commission for a poetry project about San Francisco women labor organizers. Her short stories are on the on-line magazines *Caveat Lector* and *So To Speak*. In 2018, she was a finalist in the Dora and Alexander Raynes Poetry Competition by *Jewish Currents*.

Originally from New York State, she has been living in San Francisco since 1971. She has a degree in Anthropology from Grinnell College, MAs in English: Concentration Creative Writing and Drama from San Francisco State University, and a Certificate in Labor Studies from City College, San Francisco. She is a Co-editor of the *Haight Ashbury Literary Journal*. Alice reads her poetry at Bird and Beckett Bookstore, and in the San Francisco Public Library.

www.ingramcontent.com/pod-product-compliance
Lightning Source LLC
Chambersburg PA
CBHW032024090426

42741CB00006B/729